BMW X6 M

Kevin Walker

rourkeeducationalmedia.com

TABLE OF CONTENTS

The "M" badge on the X6 M door seal.

The Sports Activity Coupe

BMW makes some of the best high-performance cars in the world. The BMW X6 M is one of BMW's most **innovative** creations.

The X6 M combines a sports utility vehicle (SUV) with a sports car. BMW calls it a "sports activity coupe." By any name, it's one of the coolest, fastest vehicles on the road.

BMW stands for Bavarian Motor Works. The company is located in Munich, Germany. In German, the name of the company translates to "Bayerische Motoren Werke." Its motto is: "The ultimate driving machine."

BMW has a long history of amazing engines and vehicles. That includes airplane engines and racing engines for motorcycles and cars.

While famous for its power, speed, and great handling, the X6 M is also simply beautiful.

R32 motorcycle, the first BMW motor vehicle.

BMW started making engines in 1917 and cars in 1928. The first cars were for the Austin Motor Company in Great Britain, but BMW started using its own designs in 1932.

A CLASS BY ITSELF

BMW calls the X6 M an **iconoclast**. No SUV is like it. As with all BMWs, it features advanced technology. But with an M-class engine, it handles the road like a sports car.

The famous BMW logo adorns the front. Side vents allow for air flow over the engine. It also has a rear spoiler to direct air flow and improve **traction**.

The famous BMW logo uses the blue and white colors of the Bavarian flag. In the late 1920s, the logo appeared as a rotating propeller in BMW advertisements. The company has used some form of that look ever since.

rear spoiler
MA1514
SOUTH CAROLINA

The rear features two pairs of dual exhaust pipes. The X6 M looks more at home on a race track than a city street!

The X6 M also has a body built to absorb the twists and turns of the road. That's why it doesn't feel like driving a big SUV.

German cars are known for high performance and the latest technology. The first modern car—the Mercedes—was built in Germany in 1901. The "Big Three" automakers in Germany are BMW, Mercedes-Benz, and Volkswagen, which makes both Audi and Porsche.

TURBO CHARGED POWER

The engine's a beauty, too. The M TwinPower Turbo V-8 blasts the X6 M from zero to 60 miles (96.5 kilometers) per hour in four seconds! That's more Batmobile than SUV, but it's what makes a BMW a BMW.

Part of what gives the X6 M its rocket-like power are the twin turbos. Turbo engines **compress** air to increase power.

BMW's patented cross-bank exhaust manifolds make the X6 M's engine a "hot V."

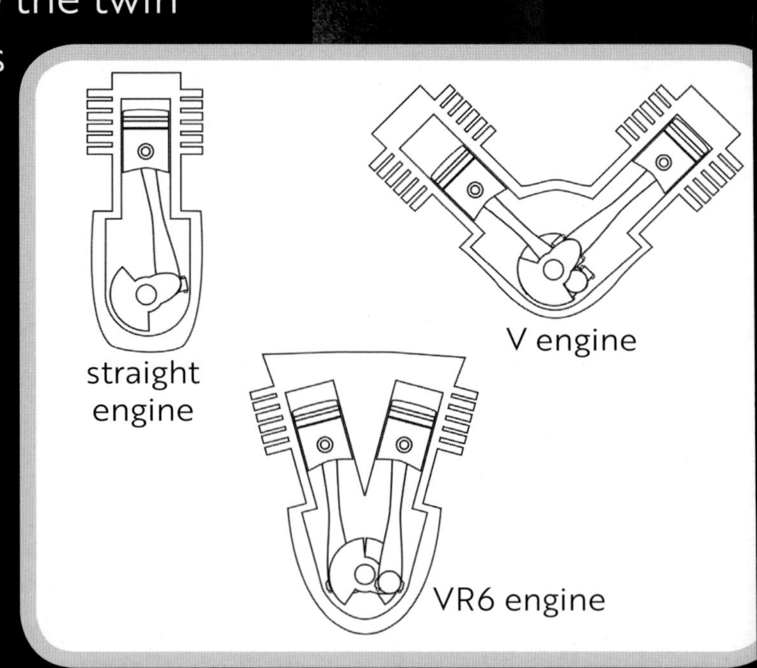

BMW M

High Tech Beauty

BMW excels at luxury. The inside of the X6 M features leather seats, a leather-wrapped steering wheel, and chrome trim.

The X6 M cabin tilts all controls toward the driver, like a race car. Drivers can change gears with buttons on the steering wheel.

The technology features include a touchscreen infotainment system, self-parking, and a 360-degree camera.

The X6 M can project the speed of the car and other information directly onto the windshield, so the driver doesn't have to look down.

In the United States, BMWs have been popular for many years. Three of the top-selling luxury cars in 2016 in the U.S. were BMWs. Three others also came from German carmakers Audi and Mercedes-Benz.

touchscreen

X Series and M Timeline

This BMW 3.0 CSL won the European Touring Car championship.

1972: BMW creates the M division (M for "motorsport") to make race car engines.

1973: The first M car, the 3.0 CSL, wins the European Touring Car Championship.

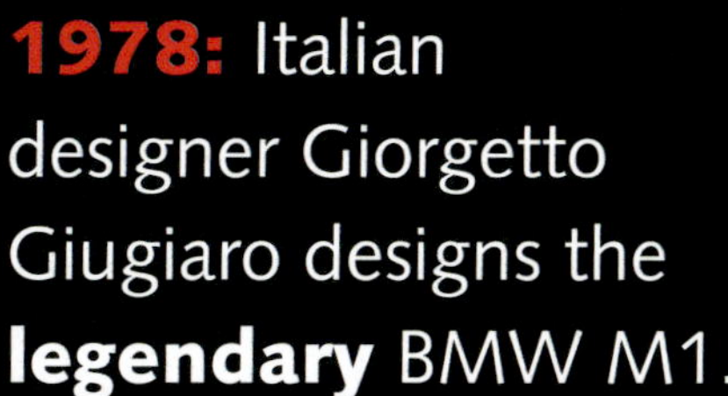

1978: Italian designer Giorgetto Giugiaro designs the **legendary** BMW M1.

Giorgetto Giugiaro was named Car Designer of the Century in 1999.

The hand-built BMW M1. Only 453 were built.

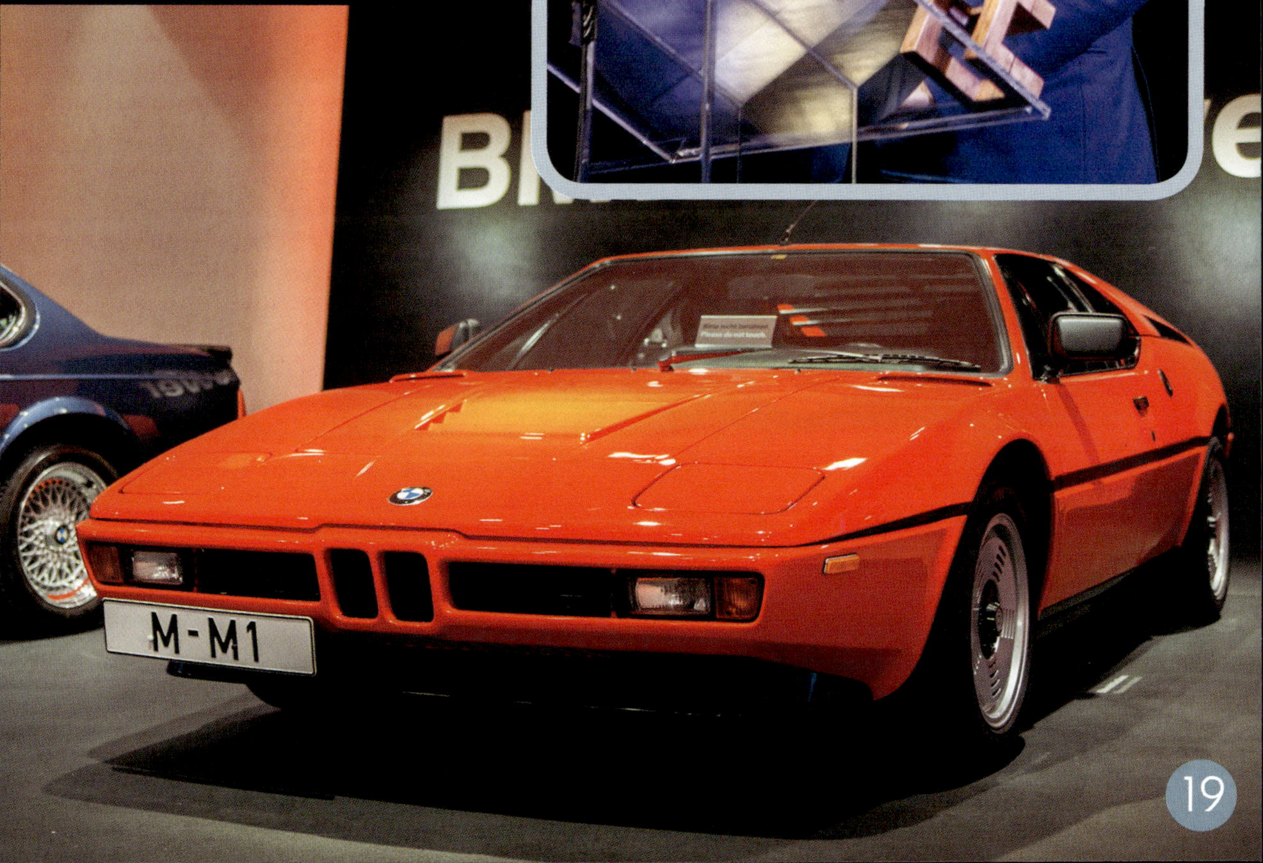

1979: BMW makes the M535i. It opens the door to combining racing engines with other types of cars.

1980s: The popularity of SUVs such as the Jeep Cherokee takes off in the United States.

The M535i combined a powerful "M" racing engine with a family sedan.

MINI Countryman

BMW also makes the MINI, a popular small car. MINI has its own SUV called the Countryman. Both BMW and MINI sales hit record levels worldwide in 2017.

1999: BMW creates the X5 SUV. It combines sports car handling with off-road capabilities.

With the X5, BMW launched the X-series of SUVs. But since BMW puts **emphasis** on performance, they call them "sports activity vehicles."

2003: The X3 series is launched. The SUV is based on the very popular 3-series sedan.

BMW X6

2008: The X6 series is released, featuring a sporty look and a higher **performance** engine than any X-series vehicle.

BMW launches a second version of the X6 with a more powerful engine.

BMW now makes six X-series vehicles, with the X7 about to be released. Only the X5 and X6 come in M versions. One in every four BMW sold worldwide is from the X-series.

The BMW X5 Security Plus can withstand attacks from guns and even explosives.

THE BMW MUSEUM

Located in Munich, the BMW Museum offers a **fantastic** collection of history about BMW vehicles, including the X-series and X6 M.

It also includes models of roadsters, racing cars, and every other kind of BMW. It's open to the public and is a must-see if you ever visit Munich!

GLOSSARY

compress (kuhm-PRES): to press or flatten something in order to fit it into a smaller space

emphasis (EM-fuh-sis): importance given to something

fantastic (fan-TAS-tik): terrific or wonderful

iconoclast (eye-KAHN-uh-klast): a person who attacks settled beliefs or institutions

innovative (in-uh-VAY-tive): a new idea or invention

legendary (LEJ-uhn-der-ee): very well known, usually because of some remarkable event or action

performance (pur-FOR-muhns): the way something works, compared to a standard

traction (TRAK-shuhn): the force that keeps a moving body from slipping on a surface

INDEX

SHOW WHAT YOU KNOW

1. In what country was BMW founded?
2. What does BMW stand for?
3. Why did BMW create the M division?
4. What was the first BMW SUV?
5. Where is the BMW Museum located?

FURTHER READING

Lewin, Tony, *The BMW Century,* Motorsports, 2016.
Braun, Andreas, *BMW: 100 Masterpieces,* Hirmer, 2017.
Road and Track, *Iconic Cars: The BMW M Series,* RosettaBooks, 2015.

ABOUT THE AUTHOR

Kevin Walker is the author of books about cars, science, and technology. He also writes about politics, film, and books. He likes books and cars the best. He's never owned a BMW, but he once owned (and loved) another German car—a 1971 Volkswagen Beetle.

Meet The Author!
www.meetREMauthors.com

www.rourkeeducationalmedia.com

PHOTO CREDITS: Credits: BWM Cars, BMW Group unless otherwise stated. Cover © UWE FISCHER; Header art © Petrosg; speedometer art © didis both from Shutterstock.com; Pg4-5; shutterstock.com - Ivan Svyatkovsky; Pg6-7; BMW_P90045832, BMW_BIKE -https://creativecommons.org/licenses/by-sa/4.0/deed.en Stahlkocher -GFDL; PG8-9 BMW_P90166922, logo © Shutterstock.com - rvlsoft; PG 12 engine illustration © Azure.km https://creativecommons.org/licenses/by/3.0/deed.en PG 16-17 © Sergey Rudavin—Shutterstock.com PG18 © Lothar Spurzem https://creativecommons.org/licenses/by-sa/2.0/de/deed.en PG 19 Giugiaro © Mitjagodnic https://creativecommons.org/licenses/by-sa/4.0/deed.en M1 © Roman Vukolov—Shutterstock.com PG 20-21 M535i © Beemwej https://creativecommons.org/licenses/by-sa/3.0/deed.en Page 21 Mini © Teddy Leung—Shutterstock.com Page 22-23 © Max Earey—Shutterstock.com; PG 24 © IFCAR, PG25 © OSX; PG 26-27 © Gyuszko-Photo—Shutterstock.com PG 28 Museum exterior © meunierd and interior © Roman Vukolov both from Shutterstock.com:

Edited by: Keli Sipperley

Cover design by: Rhea Magaro-Wallace

Library of Congress PCN Data

BMW X6 M / Kevin Walker
(*VROOM!* Hot SUVs)
ISBN 978-1-64156-480-9 (hard cover)
ISBN 978-1-64156-606-3 (soft cover)
ISBN 978-1-64156-720-6 (e-Book)
Library of Congress Control Number: 2018930700

Rourke Educational Media
Printed in the United States of America, North Mankato, Minnesota